DK Life Stories

Jane GOODALL

by Libby Romero

Illustrated by Charlotte Ager

Senior Editor Shannon Beatty
Designer Charlotte Jennings

Project Editors Olivia Stanford, Kritika Gupta
Senior Editor Roohi Sehgal
Senior Designer Joanne Clark
Project Art Editor Rashika Kachroo
Assistant Art Editor Simran Lakhiani
Jacket Coordinator Issy Walsh
Jacket Designer Dheeraj Arora
DTP Designers Sachin Gupta, Ashok Kumar
Picture Researcher Sakshi Saluja
Pre-Producer Sophie Chatellier
Senior Producer Amy Knight
Managing Editors Laura Gilbert, Monica Saigal
Deputy Managing Art Editor Ivy Sengupta
Managing Art Editor Diane Peyton Jones
Delhi Team Head Malavika Talukder
Creative Director Helen Senior
Publishing Director Sarah Larter

Subject Consultant Dale Peterson, PhD
Literacy Consultant Stephanie Laird

First published in Great Britain in 2019 by
Dorling Kindersley Limited
80 Strand, London, WC2R 0RL

Copyright © 2019 Dorling Kindersley Limited
A Penguin Random House Company
10 9 8 7 6 5 4 3 2 1
001–314130–August/2019

A CIP catalogue record for this book
is available from the British Library.
ISBN: 978-0-2413-7788-8

Printed and bound in China

A WORLD OF IDEAS:
SEE ALL THERE IS TO KNOW

www.dk.com

Dear Reader,

Interest. Dream. Passion. Mission. These are just four simple words, but if you put them together – and follow a path as you travel from one step to the next – great things can happen. Just take a look at Jane Goodall.

As a young child, Jane had an interest in animals. She dreamed of going to Africa to study wild animals. That dream came true, and Jane has spent her life fulfilling a passion that turned into a mission after she saw problems and realized that she could really make a difference.

Undertaking a mission isn't always easy, but sometimes it's necessary. If you see somebody doing something you think is wrong, speak up. Your words have power, and even the biggest changes can start with a simple conversation. As Jane once said, "If we all start listening and helping, then surely, together, we can make the world a better place for all living things. Can't we?"

Happy reading,

Libby Romero

The life of...
Jane **Goodall**

1

The **early** years

From the beginning, Valerie Jane Morris-Goodall loved animals. Big or small, slimy or soft, feathered or scaly, they were all Jane's friends.

Jane was born on 3 April 1934 in London, England. For the first year of her life, she and her family lived there on the second floor of a small, brick, two-bedroom townhouse. The ground floor, which had once been a stable, was the perfect place for her father's garage.

Jane's father, Mortimer, worked as an engineer for a company that was laying telephone cables throughout England. Mortimer's favourite part of the job was getting to travel. This meant he could drive the company van. Mortimer's mother had taught him how to drive when he was 14, and after that, driving had become his passion. He was determined to become a racing car driver.

Jane's mother, Margaret Myfanwe Joseph, who everyone called Vanne (pronounced "Van"), had moved to London from her family home in the English seaside town of Bournemouth. Though Vanne

found work as a secretary, she loved to write and actually wanted to be an author.

Vanne and Mortimer met each other in London, and then in

1932, they got married. At first their life together was a whirl of action as they travelled around Europe following the racing circuit. That focus didn't change – at least for Mortimer – after Jane was born. He was absent more often than not as she was growing up.

However, Mortimer was there for his daughter's first birthday, and the present he gave her had a lasting effect on her life. In search of a soft, cuddly toy for Jane, he found a stuffed toy chimpanzee. It was named Jubilee after the first captive-born chimpanzee that had ever been born at London Zoo. Family friends thought the toy was scary and would give little Jane nightmares.

JANE'S LAST NAME

As the youngest of three brothers, Jane's grandfather, Reginald Goodall, wasn't allowed to help run the family printing business. So when he married Elizabeth Morris against the family's wishes, he decided to make a point. Their children's last name would be Morris-Goodall.

Baby Jane cuddling Jubilee.

That wasn't the case at all – Jane loved Jubilee and wanted to take him wherever she went.

Even as a baby, Jane loved animals. In London, her nanny, or babysitter, Nancy Sowden, used to take her for long walks, and Jane loved watching the animals that scurried through the city parks. After the family moved to a larger home, Jane and Nanny (which was what Jane called Nancy) had long picnics in the overgrown garden.

Jane loved all the flowers, birds, and insects
that lived in the garden, but earthworms were
her favourite. She loved them so much that
she took a few to bed with her one night
and hid them under her pillow. Nanny was
horrified, so it was up to Vanne to convince
the tearful toddler that the worms would die
if they weren't returned to their home out
in the garden.

On Jane's fourth birthday, she got an
unwelcome surprise when her new baby sister,
Judith Daphne (Judy), was born. For a while,
Jane's safe little world was turned upside down.

She was jealous because the new baby was getting all of the family's attention.

There were even bigger changes in store for Jane and her family, though. Mortimer left his job as an engineer to become a full-time racing car driver, and in May 1939, the family moved to France. While France was a good base for a racing car driver, the timing of this move couldn't have been worse. By the end of the summer, rumours of spies and impending war were in the air, so the family quickly moved back to England.

The family's first stop was to visit Mortimer's parents, who Jane called "Gramps" and "Danny Nutt". ("Danny" was her childish version of "Granny".) They lived in an old house in the countryside. While there, five-year-old Jane gave everyone a fright when she disappeared one day. Everyone searched for her, and they even called the police. When Jane finally reappeared, hours later, she was exhausted, excited, and covered in straw. She told her mother that she had wanted to know how hens laid eggs. So for the past five hours she had been patiently waiting in the henhouse.

Now she knew, and she had just completed her first scientific observation.

Shortly after that episode, Great Britain declared war on Germany. The racetracks closed, so Mortimer enlisted in the military and was shipped off to France. Although he did return for short visits over the years, they were few and far between. (Jane's parents would eventually get divorced in 1952.)

With Mortimer gone to fight in World War II, Jane, her mother, and sister moved to Bournemouth. There, they lived with Vanne's mother, who Jane also called "Danny". While in Bournemouth, Jane and her family did have to make the occasional dash to the bomb shelter. Because the seaside town

P-51 Mustang

WORLD WAR II

During World War II (1939–1945), the Axis powers (Germany, Italy, and Japan) battled against the Allied nations (led by Great Britain, the Soviet Union, and the United States). More than 60 million people died in this bloody conflict, which ended after the United States dropped two atomic bombs on Japan.

wasn't near a large city, however, it was overall a safe place to spend the war years.

Life in Bournemouth wasn't dull, though. Jane's grandfather had died years earlier, so it was a home filled with women. In addition to Jane, Judy, Vanne, and Danny, there were Vanne's sisters, Olly and Audrey. Danny also rented rooms to other women. Living in this environment, Jane was never told that she could not do something because she was a girl. She was free to do what she loved, which mostly included reading books, climbing trees, and being around animals.

And there were lots of animals to be around in Bournemouth. In addition to the insects and other creatures she found in the gardens, Jane had hamsters, guinea pigs, tortoises, and a terrapin. She had cats and dogs, and she even learned how to ride a horse.

One local dog called Rusty spent most of his days with Jane. When she saw how clever he was, Jane started teaching him tricks. One day, she threw a ball out of a window and watched as Rusty ran downstairs. He pawed the door to get someone to open it, and ran outside to retrieve the ball. Jane was astounded to see that

THE ALLIGATOR CLUB

When Jane was 12, she and her friends founded a nature club called the Alligator Club. Each member had an animal name. For her name, Jane chose a beautiful butterfly – the red admiral. Jane was an organized, if not bossy, leader. She created badges, arranged outings, produced a magazine, and wrote quizzes that she demanded all members complete in a timely fashion.

Red admiral

Jane sitting on Daniel the horse, at Bushel's riding stable in Bournemouth, England.

Rusty actually remembered where she had thrown the ball!

It's no wonder that one of Jane's favourite books was *The Story of Doctor Doolittle*, the tale of a doctor with his own group of pets. Jane was particularly interested in Doctor Doolittle's trip to Africa. She started reading more books about the continent, including *The Jungle Book* and the entire series of books about Tarzan of the Apes. One day, she vowed, she would be like Tarzan and go and live among the animals in Africa!

2

A WONDERFUL invitation

Jane's love of the outdoors was equalled – if not exceeded – by her dislike of school. To her, school was dreary, routine, and outright boring.

There were bright spots, of course – Jane had a lot of friends and was one of the best pupils in her class. However, she could not see how anything she was learning would help her to achieve her dream of going to Africa.

Jane attended a boarding school, which is a school where pupils live during the school term. With just one year to go before she finished school and officially became an adult, Jane became depressed. More and more, she stayed at home, ill, and lay in bed reading her beloved books.

Then she had a biology lesson. Jane learned about heredity and evolution. She got to dissect, or cut open, a rabbit in order to study its heart and brain. She was also excelling in her English class and won an award for her writing. Suddenly, school was quite interesting, Jane's future didn't seem quite so bleak, and growing up didn't seem quite so scary.

But by the time Jane left school, she still had no idea what she wanted to do with her life – or at least, she had no idea how to achieve her dreams. Jane still wanted to study and write about animals in Africa. However, as a young woman in the 1950s, her career choices were pretty much limited to being a secretary, nurse, or teacher.

what does heredity mean? The passing of traits from parents to their offspring. Traits are determined by the genes you get from each parent.

Following her mother's advice, Jane decided to go to secretarial school. After all, a secretary could get a job anywhere – even in Africa. So Jane moved to London, and for the next 10 months, she studied shorthand, typing, bookkeeping, and writing at secretarial school.

Upon graduation, she started working at her Aunt Olly's physical therapy clinic, which helped people recover from injuries. Soon, she was offered a higher-paying job at Oxford University. However, it didn't take long for Jane to become bored with typing and filing documents. In this job, the closest she got to Africa was finding a hat for the emperor of Ethiopia when he was awarded an honorary degree.

Oxford University

So Jane left that job, too, and began working for a film production company in Oxford. There, she got to do everything from selecting music and editing film to modelling and being a make-up artist. This job was much more satisfying, but still, it wasn't Africa.

Jane started to think about a letter she had received the previous summer. A friend from boarding school called Marie-Claude (nicknamed "Clo") Mange, had invited Jane to visit her at her father's farm outside Nairobi, Kenya. Clo knew about Jane's dream, and she wanted Jane to stay for a full six months.

After confirming that the offer was still open, Jane moved back to Bournemouth, got a job as a waitress, and started saving up money for the trip. It didn't take long for Jane to become an excellent waitress, able to carry 13 plates at a time – without a tray! It didn't take her long to save enough money for the trip, either. She was ready to buy a ticket in just four months. And on 13 March 1957, 22-year-old Jane boarded the *Kenya Castle* and finally set sail for Africa.

The *Kenya Castle* docked in London.

The voyage was rough for most of the passengers, but Jane was having the time of her life. When the rocking of the ship made people feel sick and forced them to go to their cabins, Jane sat at the front of the ship because that's where it moved the most. And while the scorching Sun burned the other passengers to a crisp, Jane's skin had started to tan.

Jane finally arrived in Nairobi, Kenya, on 3 April – which was also her 23rd birthday.

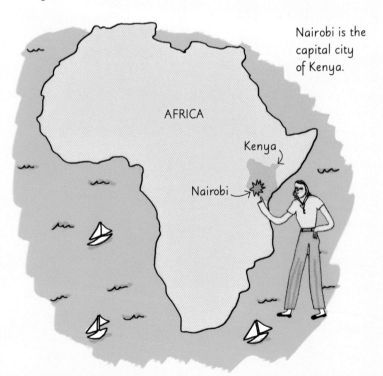

Nairobi is the capital city of Kenya.

AFRICA

Kenya

Nairobi

Chapter 3

A dream COME true

Jane was in heaven. Africa was even better than she had dreamed – and best of all, it was filled with amazing animals.

At Greystones, Clo's father's farm, there were animals everywhere. In addition to six dogs and two cats, there were cows, rabbits, chickens, and even a chameleon. When Jane and Clo went out exploring, they saw even more animals. These animals, though, were of the wild sort – hyenas, monkeys, storks, and cranes. Jane saw her first giraffe. She even got the first of her many African pets – it was a bush monkey that she named Levi.

Soon, Jane began searching for a job so she could stay in Africa. Dusting off her secretarial skills, she became a typist for a construction firm. Then, upon the recommendation of a friend, she introduced herself to Louis Leakey. At the time, Leakey was the curator, or the person in charge, of Nairobi's natural history museum, the Coryndon (now called the National Museum of Kenya).

WHO WAS LOUIS LEAKEY?

Louis Leakey (1903–1972) was a British palaeontologist, archaeologist, and anthropologist. Born to British missionaries and raised in Kenya, Leakey returned to Africa after earning his doctorate degree at Cambridge University. Working with his second wife, archaeologist and paleoanthropologist Mary Douglas Leakey, he discovered fossil remains of some of the first human ancestors. His findings changed people's ideas about human evolution and proved that the human race originated in Africa, and not Asia as people had previously believed.

Their first meeting was at his museum, and after a private tour and much conversation, he realized that she was as interested in African wildlife as he was. Leakey hired Jane to be his secretary. Before she started, though, he asked her to join him and his wife, Mary, on an expedition to search for fossils – remains or traces left by animals from a long time ago – at Olduvai Gorge in the plains of East Africa.

The Leakeys were looking for fossils of the very first humans, which they thought could be found in Africa. Jane had never done this type of work before, but she was thrilled to go with them.

Jane joined the Leakeys on their dig at Olduvai Gorge.

Towards the end of their trip, Leakey told Jane about his plan to sponsor a field study of African apes. Leakey believed that fossils could help him understand the physical evolution of human ancestors. The best way to understand how they lived and

An ancient skull, found by Mary Leakey at Olduvai Gorge.

behaved was to study apes, which are modern humans' closest living relatives. Jane was intrigued.

When they returned to Nairobi, Leakey brought up the subject again. Jane blurted out that she wished he would stop talking about his idea because it was exactly what she wanted to do. He told her that he was waiting for her to speak up because she was just the person he wanted to do it! Jane immediately agreed.

what is a field study?

A research project conducted in a natural setting instead of an office or lab. The project at Olduvai Gorge was a field study.

Leakey had already decided that the six-month study should focus on chimpanzees, and he had picked a place – Gombe Stream Game Reserve in Tanganyika (now called Gombe National Park in Tanzania). Leakey thought Jane was the ideal person for the job for a couple of reasons. One reason was that she was a woman, and he thought women would be more patient and be seen as less threatening by the chimpanzees. His second reason was that she wasn't a trained scientist. That meant her mind was "uncluttered and unbiased by theories", according to Leakey.

GREAT APES

Apes are a type of mammal with hair instead of fur, fingernails instead of claws, and opposable thumbs. Unlike monkeys, they don't have tails. There are four types of great apes: gorillas, bonobos, orangutans, and chimpanzees. The smaller gibbons and siamangs are classified as lesser apes.

Leakey sent Jane to Gombe to study chimpanzees in the wild.

Unfortunately, not everyone else agreed. It took Leakey two years to get funding for the project. The ultimate sponsor was not a big environmental organization, but Leighton Wilkie, a business owner from Illinois, USA, who was interested in human evolution.

Once that was settled, Jane had to overcome another obstacle. Officials would not allow a European woman to travel alone in this remote jungle. Jane's mother, Vanne, agreed to go with her, and they set off on their expedition.

Vanne and Jane in Africa.

"My **family** has very **strong women**. My mother never **laughed** at my **dream** of Africa, even though everyone else **did** because we **didn't have** any **money** . . .and because I was a **girl**."

Jane Goodall,
New Statesman, 2010

4

Into the **jungle**

Jane and her mother had arrived in Africa, and on 14 July 1960, they were finally given permission to make the last leg of their journey.

Travelling with a game warden and their cook, Dominic, Jane and Vanne were excited to be nearing their camp at last. It was a tough trip, though. Their vehicle was old and unreliable, the flies were unbearable, and there was the constant threat of a spillover from a violent conflict in the nearby Belgian Congo.

With the help of a regional official, they set up camp along the shores of Lake Tanganyika, one of the deepest, clearest lakes in the world.

Dominic's tent was just above the beach, and Jane and Vanne's tent was erected higher up the path in a flat clearing.

Their tent was small but comfortable. It contained a cot for each of them, along with a small bathroom at the back and a porch at the front. A bubbling stream behind the tent provided the perfect place to cool off. Nearby, they dug a deep hole, which they surrounded by a wall of woven palm leaves. It was the perfect little latrine, or toilet.

After a well-deserved night's sleep,
Jane woke up to take in her surroundings.
The land was a paradise full of animals.
On the larger side there were buffalo,
bushbucks (a type of antelope), hippos,
and, much to Jane's worry, leopards. Smaller
creatures included mongooses, squirrels, and
elephant shrews. A multitude of birds
flew through the air, and several
primate species lived in the trees.
There were also many different kinds
of snakes, a host of which were deadly.

**what is
a primate?**

A mammal with forward-facing eyes, a large
brain, five fingers, and fingernails. Humans,
apes, and monkeys are all primates.

The land was rugged and steep, and the lake sat at the base of a high plateau. Streams tumbling down towards the lake crafted steep cliffs and deep ravines that could prove impossible to climb.

Initially, the local people were suspicious of Jane's intentions and convinced that she was a spy. It took a lot of work on Jane's part to earn their trust. They were only appeased when Jane agreed to hire two local guides who would accompany her on her excursions. Meanwhile, Vanne set up a medical clinic in their camp and began treating minor ailments. This, more than anything, helped Jane establish a good relationship with her new neighbours.

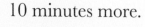

Vanne's clinic was an instant success, but Jane's guides were another matter. Jane wanted to observe chimpanzees on her own. She disliked having two extra people trail along – and trail along is what they did. Neither man could match her agile step or the endless endurance that kept her out in the jungle, searching for chimpanzees, from dawn to dusk.

For the first couple of weeks, Jane and her guides perched high on a hillside and watched a troop of chimpanzees grouped around an enormous fruit tree down below. Through her field binoculars, Jane watched the chimpanzees forage for food and recline against branches. They would even dangle by one arm for 15 minutes before, impressively, switching to the other arm and dangling for 10 minutes more.

Jane observing chimpanzees in Gombe.

By the end of July, though, the tree was stripped of its berries, and the chimpanzees moved on. Jane and her guides went on daily quests to find the troop, but the chimpanzees were elusive and Jane's companions were exhausted. Eventually, when neither man was able to go on, Jane set out on her own.

July passed, and as August took hold, the temperature grew hotter and the air became even more damp and humid. Jane, accompanied by just one guide now, continued to search for the chimpanzees. By mid-August, though, both she and Vanne had become ill.

Vanne was the first person to show symptoms, quickly registering a temperature of 40.5°C (105°F). Jane, with a temperature of 40°C (104°F), wasn't far behind her mother. After a few days of such high fevers, Dominic, their cook, urged Vanne and Jane to go to town to see the doctor, but neither woman could bear to make the trip. So, Dominic did his best to take care of them.

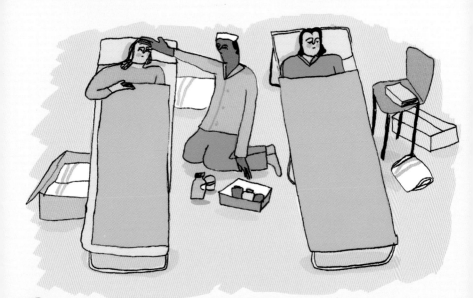

Going by their symptoms – a high fever, shaking chills, excessive sweating, headaches, and vomiting – their illness was most likely malaria. Malaria is a serious and sometimes fatal illness that is typically found in tropical or subtropical climates. Their illness kept them down for about two weeks. It wasn't until the end of August that Jane felt well enough to continue with her research.

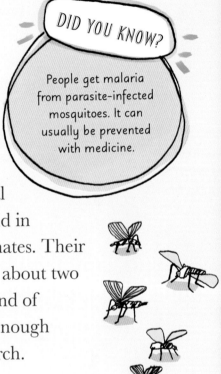

DID YOU KNOW?

People get malaria from parasite-infected mosquitoes. It can usually be prevented with medicine.

5

A big BREAKTHROUGH

Just before Jane got ill, she had an interesting encounter with a curious chimpanzee. She would later name him David Greybeard.

Ever since Jane had arrived in Gombe, she had been searching all of the faraway cliffs and valleys for chimpanzees. The search had been frustrating and produced few results, so she decided to concentrate on an area just behind her camp instead.

One afternoon, an older male chimpanzee with a silvery white beard came into the area and walked straight towards Jane. When he was about 9 metres (10 yards) away, the chimp – who seemed more curious than scared – stopped and cocked his head to one side and then the other to observe Jane. Then he scampered off into the forest.

A short while later, the chimp returned. He circled around Jane and climbed a tree so he could watch her a bit more – and then he walked away again. This was the closest she had ever been to a chimpanzee!

THE "TRIMATES" WHO STUDY PRIMATES

With the support of her mentor, Louis Leakey, Jane studied chimpanzees in Gombe. Leakey also arranged for Dian Fossey to study mountain gorillas in Rwanda and Biruté Galdikas to study orangutans in Borneo. The three women, who he called the "Trimates", revolutionized the study of primates, and how scientists observe these amazing animals in the wild.

Jane Goodall

Dian Fossey

Biruté Galdikas

Jane in Gombe,
sitting at the Peak,
where she could
observe the chimps.

When Jane recovered from her illness, she returned to the place where she had seen this curious chimp. She found the perfect place to sit and watch – a rocky perch high on a ridge that gave her an excellent view of the valley below. She called it the Peak.

Jane hoped to see more chimps from the Peak, and she wasn't disappointed. In the first five days, she saw more chimps walking, playing, and resting than she had the entire time she had been in Africa.

She also saw a leopard. Luckily, it turned and walked away.

At about this time, two trained scouts replaced the local guides who had been going with Jane on her treks. Jane was glad because these men knew how to listen for and find chimpanzees. Rather than staying together, they agreed with Jane that it would be more productive if they split up and met at scheduled times to share what they'd seen.

This arrangement gave Jane more freedom. It also, in her opinion, gave her a better chance to get close to chimps because she thought the chimps would be more likely to accept one person than a noisy group of three.

When Jane found chimpanzees, she did everything she could think of to make them feel more comfortable with her presence. She moved slowly but deliberately so she didn't startle them. She wore simple clothes in natural colours and patterns so she wouldn't distract them. If Jane sensed that she was starting to make the chimps nervous, she acted as though she wasn't interested in them at all. Sometimes, she even scratched and pawed at the ground, acting like she was just another chimp.

Still, every time Jane tried to move in closer, the chimps got scared and scrambled off into the forest. She could only study them from a distance.

Despite this, Jane was able to learn some things about chimpanzees. With her ears, she was starting to understand what the chimps' different hoots and calls meant. With her eyes, she learned even more.

For instance, she could see how the chimps moved and played. She saw how carefully the mothers took care of their infants. She saw what they ate, and she tasted fruit and nuts she had seen them eat. To learn even more about their diet, Jane dug through their poo to see what was in it.

Chimpanzees take good care of their babies.

Jane also saw the nests in trees where the chimpanzees slept, and how they used leaves and branches to build them. She even lay down in one of those nests to see what it was like. Not only was it comfortable, it was also quite springy!

Jane had been watching the chimps for a few months, and she was beginning to recognize some of them by sight. They, in turn, were starting to become used to Jane – the strange creature that had joined their group.

The truth was, however, despite all of her detailed notes, so far all she had been able to do was confirm what people already knew about chimps. This was worrying because her study was only funded for six months. Jane needed to discover something new or her work would soon come to an end. That's when David Greybeard, the first chimpanzee who had let her come close, came to the rescue.

Jane observing David Greybeard.

One day, Jane came upon a chaotic scene as she was walking through the mountain forest. David Greybeard, another chimp, and a few baboons were making a lot of noise in a tree while two large bush pigs ran around below. David Greybeard was holding something small and pink in his left hand, and from time to time, Jane saw him and the other chimp moving their hands towards their mouths.

DID YOU KNOW?

In addition to meat, chimpanzees eat fruit, nuts, seeds, flowers, leaves, and lots of different insects.

Jane watched for quite a while before she understood what she was seeing – the chimps were eating meat, most likely a baby bush pig. Before this, people thought chimps were vegetarians who mostly ate fruit. Jane had discovered something new – that chimpanzees were omnivores!

what are omnivores?	Animals that regularly eat both plants and animals. Chimpanzees are omnivores. Most humans are, too.

About a week later, Jane came across David Greybeard again. This time, she watched as he climbed on top of a termite mound, poked a long piece of grass into it, and pulled the grass back out. It was covered with termites and David Greybeard was eating them.

Later on, she saw David Greybeard and another chimp that she called Goliath strip the leaves off a twig and poke it into a mound to retrieve termites. Not only had they used a tool, but they had changed something else to make it. Scientists thought that only humans were capable of making tools. In fact, the ability to make tools was one of the traits they used to define what humans were.

FISHING FOR TERMITES

David Greybeard and Goliath were catching soldier termites with their tools. When bothered, soldier termites instinctively clamp down with their large, protruding jaws, meaning that they were attached to the tool when David pulled it out of the mound.

Soldier termite

Chimpanzees used sticks as tools to catch termites to eat.

Termite mound

Chimpanzees climbing on top of a termite mound.

"Now we must redefine 'tool', redefine 'man', or accept chimpanzees as human."

Louis Leakey,
telegram to
Jane, 1960

The discovery that chimpanzees also made and used tools was a huge breakthrough. Jane, who had been sending updates to Leakey since she arrived, wrote to

tell him about her discoveries. Leakey was astounded and quickly sent Jane a response, saying that this discovery about chimps actually challenged what it meant to be human.

Leakey set out to get more funding so Jane could continue her research. He contacted the National Geographic Society Committee for Research and Exploration, which had been supporting his own project. They gave Jane a grant of $1,400. It was the first of many National Geographic Society grants to support her studies.

6

Making progress

National Geographic's support gave Jane's work the boost it needed. Her study now had the funds it required, as well as the supplies.

One thing that did not improve, however, was the weather. It was now the rainy season in the region, and high heat and constant downpours took their toll. Books and papers were covered with mildew, and clothes and tents began to rot. A white fungus even began to grow between Jane's toes.

Depressing though all this rain was, it also led to another of Jane's exciting discoveries. One day as it started to rain, Jane saw a large group of chimps in the trees about 91 metres (100 yards) ahead. She expected them to seek shelter from the downpour. Instead, an older male chimp,

who Jane had named Paleface,
climbed down and sat in the open,
staring at Jane. The rest of the
chimps followed, and then they
divided into two groups and
started walking up the hill.

At the top of the
hill, Paleface suddenly ran
towards a bush, stood up, swiped at the bush,
turned, and charged back down the hill. As
he ran, he broke off a branch and waved
it around. Then he climbed up a tree at the
bottom of the hill. One after another,
the other chimps did the same thing.
Jane dubbed this ritual
the Rain Dance.

what is a ritual?   A set of fixed actions that are often performed
in a ceremony or as part of a tradition.
The Rain Dance was a ritual.

Jane sitting with one of her favourite chimps, David Greybeard.

As the rains continued, the trees in and around camp started producing fruit and nuts. Much to Jane's surprise, the chimps – including David Greybeard – began coming to her camp to eat. Jane could just lie in bed or in a hammock and watch them interact. As the fruit and nuts became less plentiful, Jane started offering bananas. David Greybeard loved bananas so much that one day he even stole them from Jane's tent!

HUMANS AND CHIMPS

Chimpanzees are humans' closest genetic relative, sharing about 98.6 per cent of our DNA. A common misconception is that humans evolved from chimps. That is not true. Rather, these two species share a recent common ancestor.

Jane took advantage of this proximity to learn more about the chimps – and what she saw just strengthened her earlier ideas. Chimpanzees aren't all alike. They are individuals with personalities, and they have a lot more in common with humans than was once thought. Like humans, chimpanzees live in communities or groups and each chimp has a place in that group. David Greybeard and his best friend, Goliath, were high-ranking chimps in the group Jane was studying.

Jane also learned that, like humans, chimpanzees communicate with one another. They have different calls that mean different things – and each chimp has a unique voice.

Chimpanzees also show affection. They kiss, hug, and pat each other on the back, and when they're playing, they tickle each other and laugh. They show fear and anger, and they groom each other to strengthen relationships and calm each other down when they are nervous.

By now, Jane had spent more time studying chimpanzees in the wild than any

THE "LANGUAGE" OF CHIMPANZEES

Chimpanzees use different calls and gestures to communicate with one another. For example, the sound "wraa" means fear, while "huu" indicates puzzlement. A whimper means distress; a pant-hoot, excitement; and a lip-smacking gesture shows enjoyment.

other researcher had before. As part of her agreement with National Geographic, it was time to start sharing what she had learned with the world. Jane had been taking detailed notes so she could easily write an article for the *National Geographic Magazine*. Now she needed photos.

National Geographic wanted to send a professional photographer to take the photos. Leakey insisted that the photographer be a woman. Jane didn't want anyone at all because it would be a distraction for the chimps.

Jane tried to take the photos herself, but they weren't any good. Then her sister, Judy, a novice photographer, came and tried to capture the chimpanzees on film for several weeks. Between her lack of experience and cameras breaking down in the heat and humidity, her photos were not good, either.

In all, the sisters got one good shot – David Greybeard fishing for termites on top of a dirt mound – but it still wasn't good enough to print in *National Geographic*. Because of that, the magazine decided not to publish a story about Jane and her research at this time.

Thanks to Leakey, however, word of Jane's research was getting out. Soon, she was being asked to speak at scientific conferences. She gave her first speech at the Zoological Society of London.

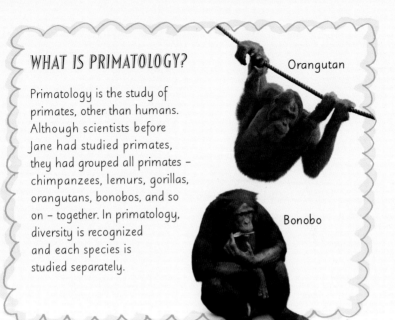

WHAT IS PRIMATOLOGY?

Primatology is the study of primates, other than humans. Although scientists before Jane had studied primates, they had grouped all primates – chimpanzees, lemurs, gorillas, orangutans, bonobos, and so on – together. In primatology, diversity is recognized and each species is studied separately.

Orangutan

Bonobo

As Jane spoke, she described what she had seen and displayed her one good photo – along with several other blurry images. The reactions to her presentation were mixed. Most people were amazed, and recognized that Jane's work was both redefining what it means to be human and creating a new field of primatology. Some, however, didn't take Jane's work seriously, since she had no formal scientific training. That, however, was about to change.

7

Dr Jane AND fame

Jane was now the world's leading expert on chimpanzees, but Leakey knew she would need a university degree for her work to be taken seriously.

Leakey arranged for Jane, who had nothing beyond a school certificate, to enroll at Cambridge University in England. For the next three years, Jane would split her time between the university and her research in Gombe as she pursued her doctoral degree (PhD) in ethology. (Ethology is the scientific study of animal behaviour.)

This arrangement was highly unusual. Not only would Jane skip the undergraduate years, but Leakey convinced Cambridge to accept the field work Jane had already done as the research required to get her

Jane studied ethology at Newnham College, an all-women's college that is part of Cambridge University.

degree. All Jane had to do was write up her dissertation in a scientific manner.

That was easier said than done. Jane had been writing detailed, precise, and accurate descriptions about what she saw. That was a form of scientific data, but the ethologists at Cambridge encouraged her to standardize her data, so it could be summarized in numbers and analysed with maths. Jane would need to learn how to think like a scientist.

What is a dissertation? A long, technical essay required to get a degree. A dissertation is written to prove someone's idea, or thesis.

Professor Robert Hinde

Jane found some of the methods she was learning to be helpful. However, she strongly disagreed with her supervisor, Professor Robert Hinde, when it came to how animal behaviour should be studied.

Traditionally, ethologists studied typical behaviours in a group. They didn't look for anything out of the ordinary, and they usually didn't name animals, as Jane had done. They gave them numbers because naming animals, Jane was told, implies that each animal is an individual. That, in turn, implies that the chimps could have humanlike traits such as a personality, emotions, and maybe even a mind.

But this, of course, was exactly what Jane believed after spending so much time with chimps in the wild. Jane refused to abandon her beliefs and decided that she knew more than her supervisors, who had never studied chimps in the wild. One day, she thought, the rest of the science world would catch on.

It was Jane's other activities during these years that opened the world's eyes to the true nature of chimpanzees. National Geographic

was still funding her research, and Jane still needed to write an article for the magazine. One thing they all agreed on at this point was the need for a professional photographer.

They chose a man called Hugo van Lawick for the job.

Hugo, born in Indonesia, was the son of a Dutch nobleman. After his father died when Hugo was four, the family moved to Australia

and then England, where Hugo grew up. Hugo
loved animals, was an excellent photographer
and filmmaker, and was dedicated to his work.
But he wasn't a woman. As some people thought
it improper for unmarried men and women to
live together, National Geographic paid Jane's
mother to return to the camp as a chaperone.

By this time, Jane had spent nearly two
years patiently making her way into the
chimpanzee community, and because of that,
her initial fears that the chimps wouldn't accept

**what is a
chaperone?**

Someone, usually an older person, who
supervises younger people in social
situations to ensure they behave properly.

Hugo van Lawick and Jane observing and filming the wildlife of Gombe.

a newcomer proved to be unfounded. When Hugo arrived, the chimps didn't retreat from him – nor did they appear startled by the sight and sound of his many cameras. Apparently, something good came out of the Goodall sisters' earlier attempts at photography after all!

Hugo's task was two-fold. He needed to take still photographs for the magazine and capture footage of the chimpanzees on film for a National Geographic documentary about Jane and her research.

To get photos, Jane located the chimps and she and Hugo went to the same place the next

GOING BANANAS

Jane started using bananas to lure chimpanzees closer after she saw David Greybeard stealing them from her tent. David wasn't the only chimp who liked bananas, though, and after a while, 20 or more chimps at a time would scour the camp searching for bananas. To keep the chimps out, Hugo had to order 13 steel boxes with lids that could only be opened by pulling a wire.

day, hoping that the chimps would return. She and Hugo arrived bright and early so they had time to build a place for Hugo to hide while Jane did her own work with the chimps.

Thanks to the chimpanzees' comfort with Jane and their obsession with the bananas she brought with her, Hugo succeeded. Jane wrote her text, and in August 1963, the issue containing a 37-page article called "My Life Among Wild Chimpanzees" went out to *National Geographic*'s 3 million readers.

Jane appeared on the cover of *National Geographic* in 1963, when her article ran in the magazine.

Suddenly, Jane was famous, and so were her chimps. Readers were charmed by Jane's description of Mrs Maggs, cuddling and playing with her baby, Jo. They felt like they knew the friendly David Greybeard and his best friends Goliath, who had a quick temper, and William, a clever thief who liked to swipe blankets, clothing, and other items from the camp.

Readers fell in love with Flo – who Jane described as hideous-looking to humans but irresistible to male chimpanzees – and her children, three-year-old Fifi and six-year-old Figan.

Readers wanted to know more, and they got their wish two years later when National Geographic's documentary, *Miss Goodall and the Wild Chimpanzees*, aired on television.

David, Goliath, Flo, and their friends were some of the famous chimps of Gombe.

Twenty million people watched as Jane led them
through the Gombe jungle and introduced
them to her chimps. Jane, who was only 31
years old, was now the most famous scientist
in the world. She was also Mrs Hugo van Lawick.

The researcher and
photographer had
fallen in love and
got married.

Jane and her husband, Hugo, getting a close-up shot of a playful baboon.

Chapter 8

Disaster strikes

Jane's research site was growing. Several buildings were constructed, and the site got a new name – Gombe Stream Research Centre.

Jane had already hired a secretary, Edna Koning, to help while she was working on her doctoral degree. However, Edna soon proved to be so good at helping with scientific research that Jane needed a new secretary. Edna, who would later conduct her own studies of baboons, stayed on to become Jane's first research assistant.

As Jane's assistant, Edna helped with observations and record-keeping. She also took part in the daily "dung swirling" duties. Dung swirling was a technique that Jane used to work out exactly what the chimps were eating. The researchers collected all of the chimp dung,

or poo, that they saw.
They put it in a tin can
with lots of little holes,
repeatedly poured water
over it, and then twirled
the can around and around
until only undigested food
particles were left.

Having someone like Edna on site
was critical because Jane was now splitting
her time between Gombe and Serengeti
National Park, where Hugo spent much
of his time photographing African animals.

WHAT IS THE SERENGETI?

Serengeti National Park is a vast ecosystem in Tanzania that covers
15,000 sq km (5,700 sq miles). Home to the biggest concentration of
large mammals on Earth, the park is famous for its great migration,
where animals battle drought and crocodile-infested rivers as they
follow the rains to find food and water.

Jane needed someone who was trained in her methods so she could supervise Gombe from afar. Jane worked non-stop on books, articles, and lectures, but she kept in regular contact with her assistants back at the camp. Some of the news was good. Three female chimps, including the beloved Flo, had had new babies. Flo's newborn was named Flint.

Other reports from camp were alarming. For instance, that summer all of the chimps became ill, and so did many of the humans. They may have had a cold, or even pneumonia. Little Flint was so ill that he didn't even have the strength to hold on to his mother. He just sat on the ground and moaned. Luckily, he pulled through.

Mother chimpanzee Flo
with her newborn, Flint.

Leakey wrote to Jane about this episode. Now that people and the chimps were in close contact with each other, and they knew that people and chimps could pass illnesses back and forth, he was worried that someday people would introduce a disease that would wipe the chimps out. Jane agreed that this was a possibility and that they should do everything they could to protect the chimps.

Unfortunately, nothing they did could stop a real disaster from striking. That autumn, some of the chimps started showing up at the camp with limp, useless arms and legs. They dragged their bodies around as best they could, but they could not move their limbs.

One chimp to come down with the mysterious illness was Mr McGregor, a grouchy older chimp that Jane had named after the farmer in Beatrix Potter's story *The Tale of Peter Rabbit*.

Mr McGregor, who had a bald head, neck, and shoulders, had been a crafty egg stealer, but now he couldn't move. At first, it was just his legs, but then one arm became paralysed, too. The other chimps attacked him to begin with, and then ignored him. The only one to stay by his side until he died was Humphrey, his best friend.

Based on the symptoms, Jane and Hugo, who were in Gombe at the time, suspected that the chimps had come down with polio. Polio is a virus that spreads orally, by mouth. It's possible that the chimps had become ill after eating food thrown out by an infected person.

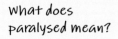

what does
paralysed mean?

When someone becomes paralysed, they lose control of their muscles. They can no longer move all or part of their body.

There was no time to waste – both people and chimps needed to be vaccinated at once. For the people, this was simple because they just had to take an oral vaccine by mouth. To vaccinate the chimps, however, the researchers had to be creative.

They decided that the best way to treat the chimps was to hide the vaccine in bananas. They used a chart to track which chimps had received the vaccine, and how big a dose each one had had. Then they waited

NO TOUCHING

Nobody at the research centre had polio, so Jane knew the outbreak hadn't started there. Despite this, she forbade physical contact between scientists and chimpanzees after this episode.

because it can take three weeks for polio symptoms to appear.

By January, the epidemic was over. Tragically, several chimps, including Mr McGregor, had died, and many more were partially paralysed. While no humans became ill with polio during the outbreak, it was a terrible blow to the chimpanzee community in Gombe. Jane and her team were deeply saddened, but were determined to move forward with their research.

9

Major changes

Jane now decided to expand her research on infant development in chimps. She was inspired, in part, by her own pregnancy.

Jane's son, Hugo Eric Louis van Lawick, was born in Nairobi on 4 March 1967. From the beginning, Jane compared his progress to that of the baby chimps she had observed in Gombe. In caring for him, Jane often used tactics she had learned from Flo, who Jane considered to be a superb mother.

Young Hugo was named in honour of three men: his father; Jane's uncle, Eric; and Louis Leakey. However, sharing a first name with his father sometimes caused confusion, particularly when Jane was writing letters home, so Jane's son got a nickname – "Grub".

Jane, her husband, Hugo, and their son, Grub, pose for a family photo.

HOW LITTLE HUGO BECAME "GRUB"

Goblin Grub was a new baby chimp in Gombe who happened to be a very messy eater. Young Hugo was even messier! Because of that, he earned the nickname "Grublin", which later was shortened to "Grub".

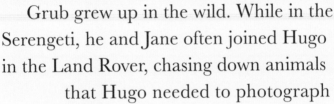

Grub grew up in the wild. While in the Serengeti, he and Jane often joined Hugo in the Land Rover, chasing down animals that Hugo needed to photograph for his assignments. They slept in tents or Jane's Volkswagen van, where they were safe from hungry predators.

When the family, or more often than not, just Jane and Grub, returned to Gombe, they stayed in a three-room hut down by the beach. The outside of the building was covered with steel mesh. This protective cage allowed cool breezes to come in, but kept chimps and baboons out of the family quarters, keeping Grub safe.

Outside the home, Jane or another adult always watched Grub very closely. The jungle and lake were full of dangers, and chimps and baboons had been known to attack human infants. As Grub got older, he learned to be cautious around the chimps, who at least once tried to grab him and run. Grub didn't love chimpanzees like his mother did, especially after one bit him on the finger!

Although motherhood kept Jane very busy, it did not slow her down.

She continued working on her research, writing, and giving lectures, which she delivered all over the world. She and Hugo worked on books together, and she wrote books of her own. One book, called *Grub: The Bush Baby*, was a children's book about Grub and the animals he saw on the Serengeti. Another book, called *In the Shadow of Man*, was an account of Jane's work with chimpanzees. It was published in 1971 and became an international bestseller.

No matter where she was, Jane always kept track of the research centre. By now, she had several research assistants and an administrator to manage the camp on site. It was from them that she learned that her beloved David Greybeard had died in the latest flu epidemic.

One of the most heart-wrenching episodes of Jane's career began when she was in Gombe.

Flo was growing old and she was weakened by the birth of her last baby, Flame. Because of that, her son Flint, who was five when Flame was born, refused to grow up.

Flint was eight and a half when Flo died, and he was so dependent on his mother that he became depressed. After his mother's death, he refused to eat and grew weaker and weaker until he died. Jane, who was away at the time, read about his death in a letter.

Jane wrote an obituary as a final tribute to Flo. Accompanied by a photograph of Flo and Flint, it was the first obituary for a non-human that was ever printed in Britain's *Sunday Times*.

Despite these losses, life went on at the research centre and new opportunities arose that ensured the centre could keep going.

DID YOU KNOW?

Louis Leakey died on 1 October 1972 – the same morning that Flo's obituary was published in the *Sunday Times*.

National Geographic had been steadily cutting Jane's grants. By 1972, she had found enough funding from other sources that she was no longer reliant upon their support.

Jane had also developed a relationship with Stanford University and the University of Dar es Salaam in Tanzania. Jane would be paid as a Stanford professor and a steady stream of undergraduate students would now be studying everything from butterflies to baboons, both in Gombe and at a facility on the Stanford campus that was to be known as Gombe West. A larger staff of African

  assistants was hired to guide the students and ensure their safety.

 Jane's personal life was undergoing major changes, too. In particular, she
 and Hugo, who were dealing with money problems and
 finding themselves pulled

in different directions at work, decided to separate. They divorced in 1974 but remained good friends.

One year later, Jane married a man called Derek Bryceson, Tanzania's national parks' director. Jane and Derek had met when he served as Tanzania's minister of agriculture. He would later go on to work in the Tanzanian government as a member of parliament.

Jane Goodall, photographed in September 1974.

10

The **darkest** years

Jane's research centre was full of activity, with up to two dozen researchers on-site. However, dark times were just around the corner.

The chimpanzee community, as they had learned, had a hierarchy of power, with an alpha male at the top. An alpha male is the dominant male in a group of animals. It was not uncommon, though, for other males to challenge his power, and sometimes they won, becoming the new alpha male in charge.

However, in the early 1970s, the main community of Gombe chimps split into two groups. Some moved

What does hierarchy mean?

A system in which people, animals, or things are ranked in order of importance. Chimpanzee communities have a hierarchy.

ALPHA TRICKS

Typically, male chimps rely on strength and aggression to rise to the top of their community. Mike, a chimp who reigned for six years, was an exception. After the clever chimp discovered that he could make a scary noise by rolling empty kerosene cans on the ground, he used this strategy to intimidate the other males.

to the southern part of their home range, while the others stayed in the north. For a while, the two groups lived apart peacefully, though the males did call and charge at each other as warnings when they met at the border.

That peace ended in early 1974 when five chimpanzees from the north caught and killed a lone chimp from the south. Over the next four years, Jane's researchers watched in horror as the northern group killed every member of the southern troop.

During these same years, the researchers discovered that chimpanzees can be cannibals. In the first instance they saw, five males from one group encountered a lone female and her baby from another community. The males attacked the female, took her baby, and ate it.

Since the chimps in this instance were from different communities, the researchers thought it was a random attack on a stranger. They were shocked four years later to learn that chimps would also attack one of their own.

What are cannibals?

Animals that eat other animals of their own kind.

The culprits were Passion, a rather antisocial chimp, and her daughter Pom. With no warning, Passion snatched an infant from its mother. She killed the infant and then shared the body with Pom. The most shocking things to Jane were that the mothers had been friends, and the motive seemed simply to be a desire for food.

Jane had seen chimpanzees become aggressive before, but it had always had a purpose, such as establishing dominance. For the most part, she had marvelled at the kindness and affection chimpanzees showed one another, so she was astonished to discover that they could also be dark and violent, just like humans.

However, that wasn't the only dark surprise Jane and her researchers encountered during these years. The second shock came when human brutality invaded their camp.

It happened on 19 May 1975, just before midnight. A long boat arrived, carrying about 40 heavily armed political rebels. They were on a mission to capture European hostages.

DID YOU KNOW?

The kidnapping only caused a one-day interruption in the continuous record of observations at Jane's research centre.

The first people they found were African members of Jane's staff. The rebels beat them and demanded to know where the *wazungu* (white people) were. Despite the threats, the Tanzanians told them nothing, so the rebels roamed through the jungle until they found the students' huts.

Eight of them managed to escape the raid, including Jane and Grub. Four students – one Dutch person and three Americans – were taken captive, though.

One week after the students were abducted, one of them was released. She carried a list of the rebels' demands: money, weapons, and freedom for their fellow guerrillas imprisoned in Tanzania.

The American and Dutch ambassadors, along with Jane's new husband, Derek, worked

What are guerrillas?

Violent fighters, sometimes armed civilians or terrorists, who attack and raid their enemies.

together to secure the students' release. David Hamburg, Jane's partner at Stanford, also came to help. Eventually, the rest of the students were released.

Jane was relieved to have everyone back, but the students' kidnapping had serious consequences for her project in Gombe. Stating that East Africa (where Gombe is located) was no longer safe, Stanford ended its arrangement with Jane and instructed its students to return to California, USA.

Daily monitoring now fell to the local Tanzanian field staff, who kept in touch with Jane via a two-way radio. Even Jane couldn't safely be in Gombe for several months – and when she finally did return, Derek and an armed guard usually went with her.

11

The **next chapter**

With Stanford's support gone and other grants becoming harder to get, Jane once again had to find funds to support her work.

The solution came while she was having dinner with friends. Jane's friends suggested that she start a tax-free charitable foundation, just as Louis Leakey had, to create a steady stream of income for her research centre. In 1977, that idea became a reality when Jane started the Jane Goodall Institute for Wildlife Research, Education, and Conservation.

Eventually, the Institute became the main source of funding for Jane's work, but she still kept busy writing and giving lectures. She even wrote another article for *National Geographic*.

THE JANE GOODALL INSTITUTE

The Jane Goodall Institute (JGI) is a worldwide non-profit organization based on Jane's vision. JGI works to protect great apes and their habitats. Its programmes also raise public awareness of environmental issues, so people will be inspired to take an active interest in the world around them.

Big changes were taking place within Jane's family, too. For instance, Grub, who had always divided his time between Jane, Hugo, and Jane's family in Bournemouth, England, was now eight years old, so his education became a priority.

When Grub was younger, Jane had sent him to nursery school in England and hired tutors to teach him in Gombe. Now, she tried to educate him herself, although she worried about teaching him spelling because she was such a bad speller! All agreed that it would be better for Grub to go to school in England and spend his holidays in Africa with his parents.

To overcome her sadness after Grub left, Jane focused on work and her life with Derek. She returned to Gombe for several days each month, but mostly managed the centre from her home in Dar es Salaam.

Then in 1980, Derek became ill. He had cancer, and the doctors said he had just three months to live. Despite Jane's attempts to find a cure, the doctors were right. Derek died three months after he was first diagnosed.

Jane threw herself into her work, and finally, she found comfort in the forests and chimps of Gombe. As she grew stronger, so did her Institute. Gordon Getty, the Institute's president,

ODE TO A PIG

Jane's mother, Vanne, underwent emergency heart surgery shortly after Derek died. Doctors replaced one of her heart valves with a valve taken from a pig. The surgery was a success, and Vanne felt better than she had in years. Jane was so grateful to the pig that had died to save her mother's life that she wrote a book about pigs.

issued a challenge. He would match any grant up to a total of $250,000. The funds his challenge raised meant that the Jane Goodall Institute at last had the money it needed and was financially secure.

Jane now had time to focus on something besides raising money, and she knew exactly what she wanted to do. Jane wanted to help all of the chimps that were held in zoos, and in 1984, she launched her new project, ChimpanZoo.

Jane had shown people through her research that chimpanzees are intelligent, sensitive, and social animals with many humanlike qualities. Yet in zoos, chimps faced prison-like conditions as they were held in cages with steel bars and concrete floors. They were often housed alone, with no one to play with and nothing to do. Jane hoped to change these conditions with ChimpanZoo.

DID YOU KNOW?

Jane couldn't get funding, so she paid for the first year of the ChimpanZoo project using her own money.

Jane had two goals. Long-term, she wanted
to improve the chimps' environments with
items like toys, bedding, and nesting materials.
However, before she could do that, she had
to tackle her short-term goal – educating
the people who cared for these chimps.

Through ChimpanZoo, university professors
and students worked with zoo employees.
Together, they compared the behaviour of
zoo chimps to those in the wild. What they
discovered led to better living conditions
for chimpanzees and other animals
held in captivity.

In 1986, Jane finished writing another book, called *The Chimpanzees of Gombe: Patterns of Behaviour*. In it, Jane wrote about 25 years of her work. Chimpanzee experts from all over the world were invited to a three-day conference in Chicago, Illinois, USA, to celebrate the book's release.

At the conference, experts shared their latest research findings, but the research wasn't what everyone was talking about. People were alarmed about the tales of chimpanzees being hunted in Africa and the photographs of chimpanzees imprisoned in tiny cages in research laboratories.

Before the conference ended, 30 of the top chimpanzee experts created a new organization called the Committee for the Conservation and Care of Chimpanzees, to address these issues. Jane agreed to help pay for it through the Jane Goodall Institute and to serve as its celebrity representative.

12

Jane's work continues

Jane had reached a turning point. She wanted to give back to the animals she'd studied for so long by advocating their rights.

Many of the chimps used in research laboratories at the time were captured as infants in the wild. For every chimp caught, though, 10 others were killed. Jane's first mission was to try to put a stop to this. She met government leaders in Africa, where the wild chimps lived, and in the United States, where many of the laboratories were located. She tried to convince them to change their laws.

Jane then set her sights on research laboratories that used chimps and other primates in their experiments. The photos Jane had seen at the Chicago conference were upsetting. But after she watched a video –

secretly made by animal rights activists who had broken into a lab – she was heartbroken.

Jane went to see the facility for herself. The chimps were housed all alone in small, prison-like cages. They were given nothing to play with, and the cages were lined up in a way that the chimps couldn't even see one another. A fan, set up to stop the spread of airborne viruses, blew into the cages and the constant whooshing sound it created was the only thing the chimps could hear. Some chimps sat motionless, while others rocked from side to side. All of them were depressed.

DID YOU KNOW?

After reading a book about animal factory farming, Jane decided to become a vegetarian.

"I spent years and years doing what I wanted to do most of all – being with wild, free chimpanzees in the forest. Now is my paying-back time."

Jane Goodall,
My Life With the Chimpanzees, 1996

After this tour, Jane visited research laboratories all over the world. She gave lectures and her Institute sponsored workshops and seminars where experts wrote a set of guidelines that would create humane conditions for the chimps held in captivity.

Jane had found ways to help chimps in zoos and laboratories. Now she wanted to help the rest, so she started the Tchimpounga Chimpanzee Rehabilitation Centre in Congo. It opened in 1991 as a safe haven, or space, for 25 orphans, badly treated pets, and former zoo exhibits, and it has taken in hundreds of chimpanzees ever since.

Jane realized that educating others would be the key to her success, so she wrote more books, gave more interviews, and was the subject of more films. Then she began to focus on educating children – after all, they are Earth's next generation of caretakers! Jane spoke about conservation to a variety of youth groups.

DID YOU KNOW?

Today, there are thousands of Roots & Shoots groups in nearly 100 countries.

During one talk in Tanzania, Jane and the children discussed problems in their community. The students were so eager to help that they started their own conservation group – Roots & Shoots. Jane's Institute became its sponsor.

By 1994, it had become clear that the destruction of forests (deforestation) around Jane's research site at Gombe was a major problem. It resembled a forest island surrounded by dirt.

Jane working with children from Roots & Shoots.

So Jane started the Lake Tanganyika Catchment Reforestation and Education (TACARE) project to educate villagers and encourage them to conserve natural resources. Since it started, villagers have planted millions of trees and worked to preserve the land. The programme has expanded to include scholarships for students, as well as better schools, medical facilities, and health education programmes.

REASONS FOR HOPE

In 1999, Jane published a book called *Reason for Hope: A Spiritual Journey*. In the book, which quickly became a *New York Times* bestseller, Jane identified four reasons for hope for the future: the human brain; the strong human spirit; the resilience of nature; and the determination of young people. Since its publication, she has added a fifth reason to her list – social media – which has the power to reach people from all around the world.

Jane won the UNESCO Gold Medal for her life's
work protecting Africa's endangered apes.

The Minerva Award, which Jane
won, honours the achievements
of remarkable women.

Jane was given the Two Wings
Award for her work to protect
and conserve chimps.

Over the years, Jane has received numerous awards and honorary degrees for her work, including the Kyoto Prize, the National Geographic Society's Hubbard Medal, the French Legion of Honour, and the Gandhi-King Award for Nonviolence. Jane has also been given the UNESCO Gold Medal Award, the Minerva Award, and the Two Wings Award, to name just a few.

Jane has served as a United Nations Messenger of Peace and was also made a Dame of the British Empire by Queen Elizabeth II. She continues to work to protect animals and our planet.

Her original research project has grown into a global organization, with offices all over the world – but don't count on finding Jane in any of those offices! You're much more likely to see her engaging with communities all over the world. Jane still travels for up to 300 days a year, giving lectures, visiting school and community organizations, and meeting Roots & Shoots groups.

Much has changed since Jane first entered the Gombe forest. Researchers now have high-tech tools to help with their studies, and people everywhere recognize the value of learning about and understanding chimpanzees, our closest living relatives. Children, inspired by Jane, are working together to build a better future. And Jane, as busy as ever, continues to spread the message she so strongly believes: "Every individual matters, whether human or animal. Every individual can make a difference."

Jane's
family tree

Reginald Goodall
1871–1916

Elizabeth
"Danny Nutt" Morris
1880–1952

Grandmother

↖ Reginald was
the youngest of
three brothers.

Mortimer
Morris-Goodall
1907–2001

First
husband

Father

Hugo van Lawick
1937–2002

Valerie Jane
Morris-Goodall
(Jane Goodall)
1934–

Son

Hugo "Grub" Eric
Louis van Lawick
1967–

110

William Joseph
1859–1921

Elizabeth "Danny" Hornby Joseph
1879–1976

Mother

Margaret "Vanne" Myfanwe Joseph
1906–2000

Judy was born on Jane's fourth birthday!

Sister

Judith "Judy" Daphne Morris-Goodall
1938–

Second husband

Derek Bryceson
1928–1980

Timeline

Jane travels to Kenya and meets Louis Leakey, who gives her the opportunity to study apes.

Jane Goodall is born in London, England, on 3 April.

Jane discovers that chimps eat meat and make and use tools.

1934

1939–1945

1957

1960

World War II occurs. Jane's father goes to fight for the British military, and Jane and her mother and sister move to Bournemouth, England.

Jane goes to Gombe Stream Game Reserve (now Gombe National Park) with her mother to begin her study.

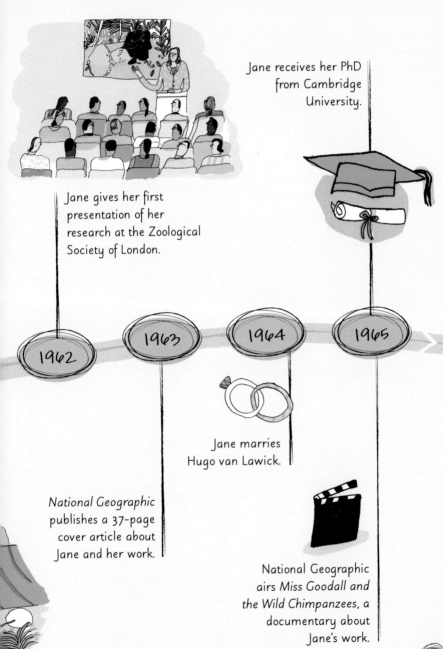

Jane gives her first presentation of her research at the Zoological Society of London.

Jane receives her PhD from Cambridge University.

1962

1963

1964

1965

Jane marries Hugo van Lawick.

National Geographic publishes a 37-page cover article about Jane and her work.

National Geographic airs *Miss Goodall and the Wild Chimpanzees*, a documentary about Jane's work.

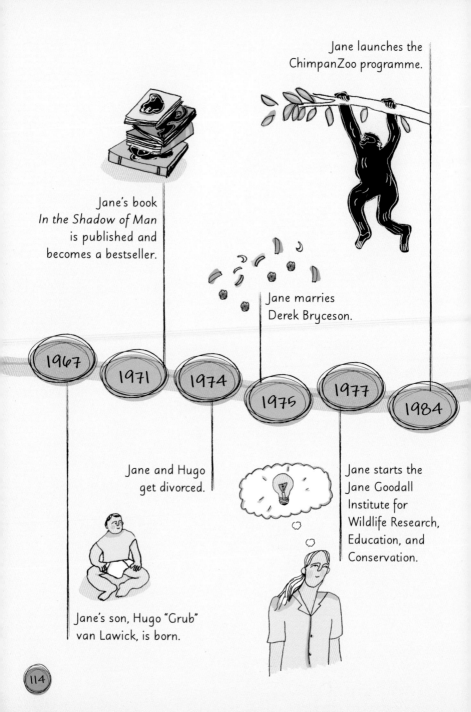

Jane launches the ChimpanZoo programme.

Jane's book *In the Shadow of Man* is published and becomes a bestseller.

Jane marries Derek Bryceson.

1967

1971

1974

1975

1977

1984

Jane and Hugo get divorced.

Jane starts the Jane Goodall Institute for Wildlife Research, Education, and Conservation.

Jane's son, Hugo "Grub" van Lawick, is born.

National Geographic releases *Jane*, a new documentary about Jane's early life and work.

The Committee for the Conservation and Care of Chimpanzees is formed; Jane becomes an animal rights advocate.

Jane becomes a United Nations Messenger of Peace.

1986

1991

1994

2002

2017

Jane opens the Tchimpounga Chimpanzee Rehabilitation Centre in Congo and begins the Roots & Shoots programme for children.

Jane starts the Lake Tanganyika Catchment Reforestation and Education (TACARE) project.

Quiz

 1 What was the name of the stuffed toy chimpanzee that Jane had as a child?

 2 What was Jane's dream when she finished school?

 3 Who gave Jane her first chance to study chimpanzees in Africa?

 4 How do people get malaria?

 5 What big discoveries did Jane make by observing David Greybeard?

 6 Where did Jane give her first speech at a scientific conference?

 7 Ethology is the scientific study of what?

Do you remember what you've read?
How many of these questions about
Jane's life can you answer?

8 What crippling human disease did the Gombe chimps start coming down with?

9 What was Jane's son's nickname?

10 What shocking, violent trait did Jane learn about chimps in the 1970s?

11 What is the name of the worldwide non-profit organization that Jane founded?

12 What did Jane realize would be the key to success for helping chimps in the future?

Answers on page 128

Who's who?

Bryceson, Derek
(1928–1980) Tanzania's national parks' director and Jane's second husband

Fossey, Dian
(1932–1985) studied mountain gorillas in Rwanda; one of Louis Leakey's "trimates"

Galdikas, Biruté
(1946–) studied orangutans in Borneo; one of Louis Leakey's "trimates"

Getty, Gordon
(1933–) philanthropist and early supporter of the Jane Goodall Institute

Goodall, Reginald
(1871–1916) Jane's grandfather on her father's side

Hamburg, David
(1925–) Jane's work partner at Stanford University

Hinde, Robert
(1923–2016) Jane's PhD supervisor at Cambridge University

Joseph, Audrey
(dates unknown) Jane's aunt

Joseph, Elizabeth "Danny" Hornby
(1879–1976) Jane's grandmother on her mother's side

Joseph, Olwen "Olly"
(dates unknown) Jane's aunt

Joseph, William
(1859–1921) Jane's grandfather on her mother's side

Joseph, William Eric
(dates unknown) Jane's uncle

Koning, Edna
(dates unknown) Jane's first secretary and first research assistant, who later conducted her own studies of baboons

Leakey, Louis
(1903–1972) palaeontologist, archaeologist, and

anthropologist; curator of Nairobi's natural history museum. Worked with his wife, Mary, to discover fossil remains of some of the first human ancestors

Leakey, Mary Douglas (1913–1996) archaeologist and palaeoanthropologist. Worked with her husband, Louis, to discover fossil remains of some of the first human ancestors

Mange, Marie-Claude "Clo" (dates unknown) friend who invited Jane to her family's farm in Nairobi, Kenya

Morris, Elizabeth "Danny Nutt" (1880–1952) Jane's grandmother on her father's side

Morris-Goodall, Margaret "Vanne" Myfanwe (1906–2000) Jane's mother

Morris-Goodall, Judith "Judy" Daphne (1938–) Jane's sister

Morris-Goodall, Mortimer (1907–2001) Jane's father

National Geographic Society organization that supported Jane's research during the earlier years

Sowden, Nancy "Nanny" (dates unknown) Jane's nanny as a young child in London

van Lawick, Hugo (1937–2002) professional wildlife photographer and Jane's first husband

van Lawick, Hugo "Grub" Eric Louis (1967–) Jane and Hugo's son

Wilkie, Leighton (1900–1993) Illinois business owner who sponsored Jane's first project in Gombe

Glossary

alpha male
the dominant male in a group of animals

anthropologist
scientist who studies humans and their societies

ape
type of primate with flexible shoulder joints and no tail – features that make it easy to swing between tree branches

archaeologist
scientist who studies the remains of things humans made and left behind, like tools, jewellery, and buildings

baboon
type of monkey

boarding school
school where students live during the school term

bonobo
type of great ape

cannibals
animals that eat other animals of their own kind

chaperone
someone, usually an older person, who supervises younger people in social situations to ensure they behave properly

chimpanzee
type of great ape

curator
person in charge of the exhibits at a museum

deforestation
cutting down or burning all the trees in an area

dissect
to cut open and separate into pieces for scientific examination

dissertation
long, technical essay required to get a degree

dung swirling
technique where researchers collect chimp poo, put it in a can with little holes, pour water over it, and twirl it until only undigested food particles are left

epidemic
quickly spreading outbreak of disease

ethology
scientific study of animal behaviour

evolution
process by which new species or populations develop through successive generations

field study
research project conducted in a natural setting instead of an office or laboratory

fossils
hardened remains of
plants or animals from
a long time ago

**Gombe Stream
Game Reserve**
park in Tanzania
where Jane Goodall
started her research;
now called Gombe
National Park

gorilla
type of great ape

grant
gift of money for a
particular purpose

great apes
gorillas, bonobos, orangutans,
and chimpanzees

guerrillas
violent fighters, sometimes
armed civilians or terrorists,
who attack and raid
their enemies

heredity
the passing of traits from
parents to their offspring

hierarchy
system in which people,
animals, or things are ranked
in order of importance

latrine
outdoor toilet

malaria
serious and sometimes fatal
illness that is typically found
in tropical or subtropical
climates and is carried
by mosquitoes

migration
large-scale movement of
people or animals from
one place to another

obituary
notice of someone's
death, usually including
information about
their life

omnivores
animals that regularly eat
both plants and animals

orangutan
type of great ape

palaeontologist
scientist who studies the
remains of plants, animals,
and other living things
from long ago

paralysed
when someone loses control
of their muscles and can no
longer move all or part of
their body

plateau
large, flat area of land
that is raised high above
the land next to it

polio
infectious disease that can
result in weakness, paralysis,
and sometimes death

predator
animal that hunts and kills
other animals

primate
mammal adapted to life
in the trees with forward-
facing eyes, a large brain,
grasping hands, and
fingernails instead of claws

primatology
scientific study of primates,
other than humans

ravine
narrow valley with
steep sides

ritual
set of fixed actions that
are often performed in
a ceremony or as part
of a tradition

Serengeti National Park
vast ecosystem in Tanzania
that covers 14,760 square km
(5,700 square miles) and
is home to the biggest
concentration of large
mammals on Earth

vaccine
substance, usually
containing killed or
weakened bacteria
or viruses, that is given
to protect against a
particular disease

Index

Acknowledgements

DK would like to thank: Marie Greenwood for additional editorial help; Jacqueline Hornberger for proofreading; Helen Peters for the index; Emily Kimball, Nishani Reed, and Nicola Evans for legal advice; Dr Dale Peterson for his expertise on Jane's life and work; Stephanie Laird for literacy consulting; Noah Harley for serving as our "Kid Editor"; and Victoria Pyke for Anglicization.

The publisher would like to thank the following for their kind permission to reproduce their photographs:
(Key: a-above; b-below/bottom; c-centre; f-far; l-left; r-right; t-top)

11 Jane Goodall Institute / www.janegoodall.org: (t). 15 Dorling Kindersley: The Shuttleworth (tr). 17 Jane Goodall Institute / www.janegoodall.org: (t). 20 Getty Images: Ashley Cooper (b). 22 Getty Images: Edward G. Malindine / Topical Press Agency (b). 25 Getty Images: Arthur Brower / New York Times Co. (br). 26 Getty Images: Tom Schwabel (b). 27 Getty Images: Werner Forman / Universal Images Group (tr). 29 SuperStock: Thomas Marent / Minden Pictures. 30 Jane Goodall Institute / www.janegoodall.org: (b). 37 Alamy Stock Photo: Everett Collection Inc (t). 41 Alamy Stock Photo: Everett Collection Historical (bl); MARKA (br). Getty Images: Neil Selkirk / The LIFE Images Collection (bc). 42 Jane Goodall Institute / www.janegoodall.org: (t). 45 naturepl. com: Anup Shah (tr). 46 Alamy Stock Photo: Everett Collection Historical (b). 48 Alamy Stock Photo: Avalon / Photoshot License (b). 49 Alamy Stock Photo: Steve Bloom Images (b). naturepl.com: Anup Shah (t). 54 Getty Images: Jane / Barcroft Images / Barcroft Media (t). 61 Dreamstime.com: Chon Kit Leong (t). 62 Alamy Stock Photo: Jeff Morgan 05 (tl). 65 Alamy Stock Photo: Everett Collection Historical. 67 National Geographic Creative: (b). 68 Jane Goodall Institute / www.janegoodall.org: Michael Neugebauer (b). 69 Getty Images: Keystone / Hulton Archive (br). 70–71 Alamy Stock Photo: Everett Collection Historical. 73 Getty Images: Wolfgang Kaehler / LightRocket (b). 75 Jane Goodall Institute / www.janegoodall.org. 81 Alamy Stock Photo: Everett Collection Historical. 84 Alamy Stock Photo: Jonny White (cla). 87 Getty Images: Fotos International (b). 104 Jane Goodall Institute / www.janegoodall.org: Chris Dickinson (b). 106 Getty Images: Francois Guillot / AFP (ca); Dr. Billy Ingram / WireImage (clb). Rex by Shutterstock: Karl Schoendorfer (crb). 109 Alamy Stock Photo: Avalon / Bruce Coleman Inc. 111 Alamy Stock Photo: Francis Specker (bl)

Cover images: Front: Getty Images: John Mahler / Toronto Star; Spine: Getty Images: John Mahler / Toronto Star c

All other images © Dorling Kindersley
For further information see: www.dkimages.com

ANSWERS TO THE QUIZ ON PAGES 116–117

1. Jubilee; 2. to study and write about animals in Africa; 3. Louis Leakey; 4. from parasite-infected mosquitoes; 5. that chimps eat meat and make and use tools; 6. the Zoological Society of London; 7. animal behaviour; 8. polio; 9. "Grub"; 10. that they can be cannibals; 11. the Jane Goodall Institute; 12. educating others